·WHEN· ·MARRIAGE· ·ENDS·

Joyce J. Tyra

HERALD PRESS
Scottdale, Pennsylvania
Waterloo, Ontario

Library of Congress Cataloging-in-Publication Data
Tyra, Joyce J., 1938-
    Starting over / Joyce J. Tyra.
        p. cm.
    Includes bibliographical references.
    ISBN 0-8361-3587-3 (alk. paper)
    1. Divorced women—United States—Psychology. 2. Widows
—United States—Psychology. 3. Divorce—Religious aspects—
Christianity.
    I. Title.
    HQ834.T97 1992
    306.89'082—dc20   92-10901
                                                                                    CIP

The paper used in this publication is recycled and meets the
minimum requirements of American National Standard for
Information Sciences—Permanence of Paper for Printed Library
Materials, ANSI Z39.48-1984.

Unless otherwise noted, Scripture quotations are taken from the
King James Version of the Bible.

Scripture quotations marked RSV are from the Revised Standard
Version of the Bible, copyright 1946, 1952, 1971 by the Division of
Christian Education of the National Council of the Churches of
Christ in the USA. Used by permission.

Scripture quotations are from the *Good News Bible.* Old Testament
copyright © American Bible Society 1976; New Testament
copyright © American Bible Society 1966, 1971, 1976.

To
every woman who by choice
or circumstance must start
over.

Contents

*My love and thanks to Tom,
Mike, and Karen for helping me
to believe that "you can
do it, Mom," and to Joanne,
Michelle, Nicole, Jennifer, and Richard
for the sunshine they have
added to our lives.*

Author's Preface

This book is for every woman struggling to cope with the ending of her marriage. Coping is tough. I know. I've been there. In 1984 my husband, Ed, died; I had to start over. I learned that healing would not occur until I muddled through a progression of five stages that eventually led to recovery. Before my husband's death, I never heard of the recovery process. But when he died, I joined thousands of women whose marriages end with death or divorce each year. In the months that followed, I learned.

When marriages end, we pick up the pieces of our lives. After a time, like it or not, we have to begin again. That's what this book is about—endings and beginnings. For after the divorce is finalized or the death certificate is filed away, the past is over. Now starting over begins.

—*Joyce J. Tyra*
Miami, Florida

ONE

Endings: Single Again

Carole

Carole stared at her husband's anguished face. "I'm sorry, Carole, I really am," he said. "I never dreamed this would happen. Believe me, I never wanted to hurt you."

An eternity before (or was it minutes?), Carole had been scraping food from the dinner dishes when Jim, her husband of 22 years, reached across the table and touched her hand. "Sit down, Carole, please," he said. "We have to talk."

Her stomach constricted. Now Jim would finally explain the frequent late nights at work, the reasons behind his gradual, growing indifference.

For nearly a year Carole had suspected that something was wrong, terribly wrong. On evenings Jim came home from work early, she often caught him staring absently at a book. He didn't turn the pages.

When she tried to question him, his answers were

evasive, vague. "Nothing is wrong," he'd say. "There's a problem at work; I'll work it out." Then he'd retreat again behind a mask of silence.

Carole didn't understand the silence. Nor did she understand the wall growing like a cancer between them. She tried to push Jim's mysterious "problem" from her mind by pretending to Ronnie and Mark, their teenage sons, that everything was fine. But everything wasn't fine, and she knew it.

Now at last the pretending would be over. Jim was going to talk. They would talk about whatever problem they faced and solve it. Then Jim would be his old self again.

Carole forced a smile. "What is it, Jim?" she asked softly. "I know you're troubled." She read the pain in his eyes. Her stomach turned icy with fear.

Jim began to pace. "I don't know how to say this," he said. Avoiding her eyes, he took a deep breath. "Carole," he began, "there's someone else."

She shut her eyes tightly. "Someone else?"

"Yes. We met at the office two years ago." His pent-up words, finally released, tumbled faster and faster.

Carole stared at her husband's lips. Then abruptly, his words stopped. He looked at her pleadingly. "Please try to understand, Carole," he said. "I love her. I'm going to move out tonight. I want a divorce."

The cup Carole held tightly in her hands slipped and smashed against the shiny tile of the kitchen floor.

Ruth

Ruth heard John's key scrape the lock. She glanced uneasily at the clock. Her husband was drinking again;

she didn't know what to expect. She was picking at a stitch in the needlepoint on her lap when he walked into the room.

"Hey, Ruthie, still up?"

"Sharon isn't home yet," she answered. "I couldn't sleep."

John loosened his tie and slumped into his easy chair. "I need a drink, babe," he said. "Get me a beer."

Ruth held her finger to her lips. "Shh, John. Petey's asleep."

John rubbed his eyes with the back of his hand and belched. His breath stank of alcohol.

"John, you promised you wouldn't drink anymore," Ruth pleaded. "You've been sober for two months. Why now? Why do you want to start drinking again?"

John stared at her through red-rimmed eyes. "Don't start whining," he said. "I'm sick of hearing it."

Ruth sighed. Tears blurred her vision. "I'm going to bed," she said. "You're drunk. We can talk about it in the morning."

John's voice was slurred. "I am *not* drunk," he yelled. "I'll get my own damn beer."

Sharon, Ruth and John's sixteen-year-old, opened the front door, glanced sideways at her parents, then hurried up the stairs.

"What's with you, Miss High and Mighty?" John yelled. "Too good to speak?"

"Good night, Mom, Dad," she called before closing her bedroom door.

The commotion woke Petey. His light brown hair was tousled, and his pajamas hung from thin shoulders. He came into the living room carrying his soft toy dog. "Mommy," he said. "I had a bad dream. I want some water, please."

"Go back to bed, Petey," Ruth said. "I'll be right in."

"What is this?" John muttered. "The whole damn house is up. Put that toy down, Pete. You're too old to sleep with a doll."

"He's only seven, John. He'll outgrow it."

John held out his hand. "Give it to me."

"Please, Daddy, no."

"Are you deaf? I said—give it to me!"

Petey looked at Ruth and began to cry.

"You're a sissy," John yelled, his anger out of control. "Stop that stupid crying or I'll give you a reason to cry." He smashed his fist into the little boy's face. Petey crumbled into a sobbing little ball.

Ruth screamed. Before she could help Petey to his feet, John grabbed her arm and hurled her against the wall. She held her breath as he stumbled into the bedroom and passed out, face down, across the bed.

Sharon crept down the stairs. She, Petey, and Ruth huddled together in the corner of the dimly lit room. Then, still shaking and dressed in her cotton bathrobe, Ruth drove the kids to her sister's house. The following morning, she filed for divorce.

Susan

Susan was tired but didn't dare close her eyes. She couldn't. Her husband, Ralph, might wake and call her. She shifted her weight on the straight wooden chair, stood, and stretched. Then she tiptoed to Ralph's bed. She looked at his swollen face and the tubes connecting him to life.

She straightened the blanket covering his thin body and glanced at the nurse entering the room. "Why don't you get some rest, Mrs. Evans?" the nurse said. "We'll call you if there's a change."

Susan nodded. "A cup of coffee would taste good. I'll run down to the cafeteria and be back in ten minutes."

The nurse patted her arm and replaced a bag of fluid that hung above Ralph's bed.

In the cafeteria, Susan found an empty booth. As she stirred a sugar cube in a paper cup of tepid coffee, she wondered if today would be the day. Ralph looked so bad. She didn't see how he could live much longer. He'd fought the hopeless battle for over a year. Cancer was winning.

"A year at the most," the doctor had said on that heinous afternoon in his office. An inoperable tumor on Ralph's brain would end his life, their thirty-year marriage, their dreams, their future.

Ralph refused to give in to his enemy. He was determined to fight. Only fifty, he had many reasons to fight. Janine, his oldest daughter, was expecting her first child at the end of the summer. His sons, Kenny and Don, were in college. Laura, his youngest, was still in high school.

Ralph endured the nausea of chemotherapy, the vomiting, the loss of hair. He suffered the excruciating headaches and the dizziness. The months slipped away.

The last few weeks Susan watched as death crept slowly into Ralph's eyes. He slept most of the time, sedated against the enemy. Then three days ago he was admitted to the hospital for the fourth time. "It won't be much longer," the doctor had said. He needn't have told her. Susan knew.

Back in the room, Susan sat by her husband's bedside and stared absently out the window. The sky was beautiful and cloudless. In another world two sailboats drifted along Biscayne Bay.

Later that evening, Ralph's battle was mercifully over. Susan didn't cry. She couldn't. There were no tears left.

Joyce

Joyce married Ed, her tall, lanky, high school sweetheart, shortly after graduation. Then they settled snugly into "happily ever after"—complete with house in the suburbs, three children, a cat, and a dog. As the years passed, they had their share of problems. But more importantly, they had their love for each other, and they had their dreams.

But death doesn't care about love. It doesn't care about dreams, either. Accidents, heart attacks, cancer . . . all are thieves robbing victims of their lives.

Ed's killer was leukemia. It struck quickly, without warning. Almost never sick, Ed had caught a winter cold. A few days later, he was admitted to the hospital with pneumonia. Joyce was concerned but not worried. With rest and medication, she assumed, Ed would soon be well.

But he wasn't. Five days later he died.

"A quick death was merciful," the doctor said. His voice was gentle, kind. In shock, wide-eyed, Joyce and the children stared at him. Merciful? How could that be? Ed was dead.

"Along with pneumonia," the doctor explained, "Ed had hairy cell leukemia. It's non-treatable," he continued. "The duration of hairy cell is about three months, usually much less."

"But how long did he have it? And why weren't there symptoms? And how could we not suspect that he was so ill?" Joyce and the childrens' questions tumbled, faster and faster.

Helplessly, the doctor shrugged his shoulders. "We can't be sure. Probably about six weeks. That's average for hairy cell. Your husband was spared a lot of pain," he continued. "Had he lived another month, it would not have been quality time. It's hard, I know. But try to think of his death as a blessing."

"A blessing?"

"Yes. You wouldn't want him to have suffered. And he would have. Be thankful he was spared that. You understand, don't you?"

Joyce nodded. But she didn't understand. All she knew was that at forty-seven her high school sweetheart, best friend, companion, and loving husband of twenty-six years was dead. And how ironic that he died, of all days, on the day set aside for sweethearts—Valentine's Day.

Understand? No. Ed's death was a nightmare, a bad dream. How could she understand the unfathomable?

Joyce didn't know it then, but more than two years would pass before she could "understand" and accept Ed's sudden death.

I know. I'm Joyce.

TWO

... And They Lived Happily Ever After Fairy Tale

In 1984 Carole, Ruth, Susan, and I joined over eight hundred thousand widows and nearly one million divorcées who become single in the United States each year. The numbers are overwhelming, aren't they? On her wedding day, each bride stood beside the man she loved, smiled, and believed in "happily ever after." Each thought an early ending of marriage couldn't possibly happen to her. But it did.

Susan and I never dreamed our marriages would end before our twilight years. Neither suspected that in our forties she would bend over the casket of the person most dear to her. On their wedding days, Carole and Ruth never dreamed circumstances would change and their marriages would dissolve in divorce.

How could we know these things? On our wedding day, as we basked in the glow of happiness, the thought that we'd be single again in mid-life never entered our minds. This certainly wasn't the way we planned it. What happened to "happily ever after?" In the 1980s, fifty-six is the average age for becoming widowed and one of every two marriages crumble. For us and thousands of women, "happily ever after" is a fairy tale with a lousy ending.

Before 1960, divorce was far less common than today. Then it was a rarity, frowned on by most church denominations and thought taboo by many. Unless one partner had a serious drug or alcohol problem, was physically abusive, continually broke the law, denied the other the right to have a child, or committed adultery, most couples chose to remain married for the sake of the children or for religious and social approval.

This is no longer true. Today divorce strikes in homes of church members as well as nonchurch members. In research by Hunt and Hunt for their book *The Divorce Experience,* they discovered that the religiously devout used to be less likely to divorce than the non-religious. However, this is no longer evident. Church attendance is one of society's accepted indications of devoutness—and statistics show that devoutness has little to do with the number of couples who divorce. Today church members are as apt to divorce as non-church members.

It seems that sometime during the past thirty years, couples began to choose divorce to end unhappy, unfulfilling marriages rather than sticking it out for the sake of the children. Reasons to divorce became as simplistic as "we were bored with each other" or "I couldn't stand his snoring another minute."

Today divorced people make up a large portion of our society. They are teenagers and senior citizens. They are ditchdiggers and college professors. They are millionaires and people on welfare. Some are parents and some childless. Some wanted the divorce and some did not. In his book *Rebuilding,* Bruce Fisher provides a definition for the two categories of divorce participants. He calls the person who initiates the divorce the "dumper" and the reluctant spouse the "dumpee."

In her divorce, Ruth was the dumper. She initiated the divorce when she felt she could no longer remain married to an alcoholic who physically abused her and their children.

"You know, it's odd," she told me. "I felt relieved when I finally left John. But then I felt dreadful, too. We were so in love on our wedding day," she said wistfully. "I still love him. I guess I always will. But I couldn't take his drinking any more. When he was drinking, he embarrassed me in front of our friends.

"For years I made excuses for him. He promised to stop drinking, and he would stop for weeks, sometimes months. But then, without warning, he'd start drinking again. Many times he threw the dishes across the room, and one time he shattered two windows. He didn't know what he was doing.

"Later when he was sober, he'd promise it wouldn't happen again. But it always did. Then the night he clobbered Petey, I knew I had to get the divorce."

Unlike Ruth, Carole didn't initiate her divorce. Instead, she was the dumpee. Carole's was a storybook marriage with husband, Jim, two sons, and a home in the suburbs. She worked part-time as a receptionist in a doctor's office, bowled once a week, and faithfully exercised to maintain her size-twelve figure. When Jim said he loved another woman and wanted a divorce, Carole's world crashed.

"This is the thing that happens to someone else," she said. "When it happened to me, I couldn't believe it. I kept telling myself, 'It isn't fair, I'm a good wife. How could Jim fall in love with someone else?' " She shook her head and sighed. "It was terribly difficult to accept that my husband no longer loved me and wanted to end our marriage."

A divorcée—whether like Ruth the dumper or like Carole the dumpee—participates in the decision to end her marriage. But for eight hundred thousand new widows each year, marriage ends through an illness or an accident. In Susan's marriage, death crept in slowly, steadily. In my marriage death came quickly, without warning. The results were the same. Our men died and our marriages ended. We became widows.

We did what was necessary. We selected the coffins, the verses, the pallbearers. Dazed, we greeted friends at the viewing. We sat through the funerals; along with our men, we buried a part of our souls. Then we acknowledged the food and flowers with notes of gratitude and began to mourn.

Although marriage ends differently for a divorcée than it does for a widow, the outcome is the same. In her book *Formerly Married*, Marilyn Jensen points out that a widow must deal with a death *in* her family while the divorcée must deal with the death *of* her family. The point is, each of us must deal with the ending of her marriage. Each of us must start over.

Widows have the ritual of the funeral and letters and cards from friends to help us. But society has no rite of passage, no ritual to help a divorcée mark the end of her marriage. There is no cemetery to visit. Neighbors don't bring platters of food. Friends don't send flowers. Society usually doesn't extend sympathy for the divorcée, even though many are indeed grieving.

Although society has no ritual of mourning for the divorced, psychologists tell us that divorcées should also expect to experience a mourning period. As marriage deteriorates, conflict helps most divorcées to prepare emotionally for the finality of divorce. However, sometimes the emotional ending occurs many years prior to the divorce and sometimes it occurs long after the divorce papers are filed away. Either way, psychologists explain that mourning helps one accept the ending of marriage. And mourning is as normal and necessary for divorcées as for widows.

Whether the husband is lost to another woman or to death, the future that was planned is lost. It is natural to mourn the loss, the shattered dreams, and the times that were good. The fairy tale has ended. Lives have been turned upside down, and the impact is overwhelming.

Frustration, loneliness, and anger are just a few of the demons that tie our stomachs into tight little knots and cause our heads to throb. Sometimes it takes every ounce of effort just to get through each day. We feel we're on the edge and wish we could push a button, stop the world, and just jump off. We hurt, and we want the pain to stop. But it doesn't.

If your marriage ended recently, I wish I could promise your pain will diminish soon, but I'd be lying, because the pain likely will continue. Yet I can promise that the pain *will* someday ebb. Don't believe that you won't be happy again. You will. But don't expect that you'll be the same person you were before your marriage ended. You won't. The ending of marriage changes you just as surely as it changes your life.

In the early months after Ed's death, I didn't think life would ever be satisfying again. Now I know that recovery from the hurting *does* occur. It did for me, and it will for you. But you'll have to work at it. Psychologists tell us there are five stages essential to the process of recovery. By being aware that everyone whose marriage ends will muddle through these stages, you'll realize you aren't alone. Even though there may be times you will suspect you're losing your mind, you aren't. Instead, you're probably bogged down in one of the stages.

According to psychologists, whether you lose your husband to death or lose him to divorce, the stages of the recovery process are the same. The terminology is different in each of the books and articles I've read, but the concept is the same. I'll provide a brief explanation of the five stages. As you read them, try to identify the stage you're in right now.

I've struggled through each of the five stages, and I agree with the experts—there aren't any shortcuts. There isn't an easy way. I had to make a gigantic effort to work through each stage. You will too. Face it. Now that you are single again, you must start over. But how and where do you begin?

THREE

This Can't Be Happening!

Stage One: Shock/Denial

You begin in the first stage of the recovery process. The stage is called *shock/denial*. In this stage, you can't accept that your marriage is over. You're shocked, numb. Even when you know the end of your marriage is coming, you experience shock when it actually happens.

Psychologists say that "dumpees" are hit especially hard. In the early weeks after her husband, Jim, moved out, Carole used to drive past his apartment. She wanted to catch a glimpse of him with his girlfriend. She told herself that if she could just *see* the woman and Jim together, then maybe she could accept that the nightmare she was living was reality and not a horrid dream. In the meantime she kept thinking that any minute she'd wake up and everything would be fine.

"My denial was so strong," Carole said, "I'd call and beg Jim to tell me what went wrong, to give our marriage another chance. If the woman answered the phone, I'd quickly hang up, then sob myself to sleep."

Unlike Carole, Ruth was the one to file for divorce. But she experienced shock/denial too. "My marriage was over long before I left John," she said. "But because I'd pretended to myself and my friends for so long, I was not facing reality, and that's really a form of denial."

Ruth looked thoughtfully at her hands before continuing. "I think," she added, "that because I'd pretended for years before I could finally admit that my marriage was over, it was a relief to end the pretense. The years I spent denying that John had a drinking problem and that we weren't happily married were very stressful."

Psychologists explain that one of the most emotionally stressful of life's events is the ending of marriage. This is true even if the marriage wasn't good. The ending of marriage is always traumatic. When it actually happens, no matter how bad the marriage was, it's difficult to admit it's really over. Instead, the common response is denial. When we deny, we unconsciously provide time until we can accept the reality. Psychologists emphasize that shock/denial is a *normal* reaction; nature provides it as a temporary buffer against emotional pain.

"Because divorce is the death of a marriage," writes Esther Fisher in her book, *Divorce: The New Freedom*, "it is helpful for divorcées to think of their divorce in terms of death. The husband, wife and children are the mourners, the lawyers are the undertakers and the court is the cemetery where the coffin is sealed."

Psychologists suggest a little exercise to help divorcées deal with denial and the finality of divorce. They suggest putting a copy of the divorce papers into a box, then either burying or cremating the box. This suggestion may seem a bit extreme, but it helps the divorcée overcome denial and accept the fact that the marriage is really dead, over.

Widows experience shock/denial, too. But the widow's husband is dead. She knows it's final. She has no hope that something will change and he will return. Because most divorcées remain in contact with their ex-husbands, the first stage, shock/denial, is usually far more difficult for them than for widows.

FOUR

Angry? You Bet We Are!

Stage Two: Anger

Psychologists tell us that *anger* follows shock/denial. It is the second stage in the recovery process. In this stage we blame our ex-spouse, another woman, ourself, God, anything and everyone for our unhappiness.

Widows are left alone through circumstances beyond our control. We usually don't have to deal with rejection and hatred. I never felt rejected when my husband died. We don't have to imagine our husbands in the arms of other women. Most widows didn't deal with physical or mental abuse, drunkenness, or desertion.

But we do deal with anger.

We seethe at a husband's death when older or unworthy men still live. Inwardly we shout, "Why me? Why my husband? Life isn't fair! It's unjust and impossible to understand!"

We're angry at the doctors who couldn't be God.

And many of us are angry at God because we're taught that everything that happens is God's will. We wonder why God allows the unfairness of life and why good people suffer and die before a normal life span is concluded.

"Ralph was a Christian and so am I," Susan told me two years after Ralph's death. "My faith is comforting because I know that Christians are guaranteed a better life following death. Realizing this is helpful," she said. "But poor God," she added. "He must have had tired ears listening while I continually cried, 'Why Ralph, God? Why did he have to die so soon? Why God? Why?' "

She smiled, then continued, "Although I was angry at God after Ralph died, my faith in God was a great strength and comfort. I don't know how widows without Christian faith ever get through the agony."

Psychologists tell us that when a marriage ends, it's natural to be angry at the unfairness of life. It's also natural to vent our anger on the persons or circumstances we believe are responsible for our unhappiness. They tell us not to be surprised when we're angry at the people who seem to go unscathed by life, especially if we believe they are undeserving.

We also shouldn't be surprised at our anger toward friends when they tell us to "keep busy" or "don't dwell on your loss." We know they mean well but wish they'd keep their advice to themselves. Unless they've walked in our shoes, they don't understand our feelings. We don't want to hear their empty platitudes.

Although widows are angry, divorcées are even angrier. A divorcée friend of Susan told her she thinks that "widows have it far easier than divorcées because at least widows know where their husbands are." Although this is a ridiculous statement, it is true that a widow doesn't have to chase a disappearing ex-husband. We don't have to argue over child support, or deal with an ex-husband's new wife and children.

"When my marriage ended," Carole said, "anger nearly destroyed me. I hated every woman who was happily married in her safe, snug little world. I hated Jim for discarding me like yesterday's trash. I hated his girlfriend. I hated my friends who told me to 'snap out of it.' I hated the world."

Ruth smiled. "I know what you're saying, Carole. I felt the same way. I was raised to believe that marriage is for keeps. Oh, sure, I knew statistics show that at least half of first-time marriages end in divorce. But I was *sure* mine wouldn't be one of the losing half.

"After all," she continued, "my parents are still married. They set a good example. I was determined that my marriage would be every bit as good as theirs. In the beginning I bent over backward to please John. I always made sure I looked nice when he came home from work. And all our family vacations were camping trips. I *hate* camping trips! Can you believe I even went to a zillion football games and never complained, not even once!"

Carole laughed. "Sounds like you were a saint."

"Not quite. But you can imagine how angry I was when, no matter what I did or didn't do, I realized that my marriage was slipping through my fingers. At first I refused to believe it was happening, so I started pretending. I pretended to myself and to everyone that everything was fine.

"But of course it wasn't and I seethed with anger. Why did my marriage have to be one of the 50 percent doomed to failure? Of all the men in the world, why did I have to fall in love with an alcoholic? I was angry at John for destroying my childish dreams of a story-book marriage.

"Oh yes, Carole, I know *exactly* what you mean when you say you were angry. The only difference," she added, "was that my anger occurred *during* my marriage and yours occurred later."

When divorce ends marriage, anger is a natural reaction. If you've been disillusioned as Ruth was or rejected as Carole was, of course, you're angry. This isn't surprising. Who wouldn't be? However, according to psychologists, when anger controls your emotions and this anger doesn't diminish after awhile, you're harming yourself and stagnating in the second stage of the recovery process.

Try to imagine a boiling teakettle. When boiling, the steam has to be released, right? Although we're certainly not teakettles, we *are* boiling. Letting off a little steam is necessary to our health.

But don't be like a divorcée I know. Angry at her ex-husband, she followed him to his girlfriend's house. When he went inside, she let the air out of his tires. Then she hid across the street to watch his reaction when he came out. Sure, she caused him inconvenience. But was her revenge worth lowering her standards as a civilized human being? Was there a better way to let out the steam and vent her hostility and anger?

According to psychologists, there is. They explain

that anger should be dealt with constructively. Constructively? How? They suggest that we vent our angry words in letters. Then instead of mailing the letters, we should tear them into little pieces. By doing this, we're releasing our anger without resorting to spite or vindictiveness.

There is another way to handle anger and bitterness. Above all other methods, this one works the best. What is it? The answer is one word. *Forgive.*

Forgive? Yes. I'm not kidding. I don't mean instant forgiveness, cheap forgiveness. But the forgiveness that comes through setting out on a journey of little by little letting go of our hatred of others, even if it takes months or years.

When we finally forgive those who hurt us, we eliminate thinking bitterly about them. When our thoughts aren't dwelling on those we once hated, much of the pain is erased from our life.

When we ask God for forgiveness, he forgives us unconditionally. Shouldn't we try to follow God's example and forgive those who cause us pain?

"Let all bitterness, and wrath, and anger, and clamor, and evil speaking, be put away from you, will all malice: And be ye kind one to another, tenderhearted, forgiving one another, even as God for Christ's sake hath forgiven you" (Eph. 4:31-32).

FIVE

Who Said, "Big Girls Don't Cry"?

Stage Three: Depression/Guilt

Anger, when not released constructively, can be turned inward. When this happens, we are cobbered with the third stage in the recovery process. This stage is *depression/guilt*.

When marriage ends and the world is crumbling about us, depression smothers like fog. It's so thick we can't see beyond ourselves and the pain we feel. We can't run from it. We can't escape by being with friends or family. We fill our lonely hours with work or with projects until exhaustion finally allows us a few hours respite with restless sleep.

But the grief and the loneliness refuses to go away. Our days are colored gray and life is unbearable. Sometimes we feel so lonely and lost we wish we could die. But we don't. Instead, we put one foot in front of the other and somehow get through each day.

The first two years following Ed's death, I sat at the

cemetery for hours every week. I talked to him, sharing my fears and problems. I loved him; his death didn't end that love. I buried him, not my love for him.

So you see, when you say your heart is broken, I know what you mean. I understand your feelings. It's hard to live without your husband and the love you shared.

According to psychologists, grief is more intense for widows than for divorcées. Maybe this is because most of us were fortunate to enjoy good marriages, whereas many divorcées endured frequent periods of loneliness and unhappiness before their marriages ended.

The intensity may be less severe, but most divorcées suffer bouts of sadness, too. You grieve for what could have been. You grieve for the disappointment of your children. You mourn the death of a dream, a standard of living, a way of life.

Throughout sleepless nights, you stare at the ceiling as questions play ping-pong in your mind. You wonder what you should have done differently. You question why your marriage failed. How did it happen? When did the problems start? You're hurt and disappointed. Your thoughts are fragmented, disjointed. Tired and lonely, you feel degraded and discarded.

If you were "dumped," feelings of worthlessness will drive you crazy until you learn to deal with them. Psychologists warn that you must not be too hard on yourself. They explain it's too late for guilt; stop the "if onlies," because they don't count any more. Instead, learn from the mistakes. Take the new knowledge. Grow with it.

Remember—it's normal to be sad when marriage

ends. Forget what your mother told you when you were a little girl; big girls *do* cry. The release of tears is nature's medicine. After the tears, you'll eventually smile again. Until then, remember that although you may not believe it now, *the end of your marriage is not the end of your life*.

Contrary to what "dumpees" think, "dumpers" don't sail through the ending of their marriages unscathed. They have their share of depression, too. However, because most dumpers contemplate divorce long before their divorce is final, their depression occurs much earlier than for dumpees. Once the inevitable ending of their marriage is out in the open, dumpers breathe a sigh of relief. The worst is over, they think.

"Not so," said Ruth. "The old demon *guilt* soon rears its ugly head. When John became physically violent, I knew I had to stop the pretending and end our marriage.

"But I was brought up to believe divorce is failure," she said. "I didn't want to admit to my friends and family that my marriage was doomed. Most people in my circle of friends shrug off divorce as a way of life for entertainers and movie stars.

"But for average, everyday people, that's a different story. Also in the eyes of most churches," she continued, "divorce represents failure to keep God's word. I was miserable because, not only was I heartbroken, I felt John and I had failed God, too."

Ruth eventually realized that normal, respectable people find the courage to end devastating marriages. This is indeed a failure. But God works with our brokenness and redeems our failures, making us new.

The pastor of her church was wonderful. "Most church doctrines do disapprove of divorce," he explained. "But some situations may make continued marriage impossible." He told her that extreme alcohol or drug abuse, adultery, emotional or physical abuse may finally be as destructive to God's plan as divorce.

"When these situations are present," her pastor explained, "a separation is needed to protect the abused wife and her children. Professional counseling should be sought. If the errant husband refuses to accept help and continues to dishonor the marriage, divorce may be necessary."

I don't mean to minimize the tragedy of divorce or the disruption of God's plan which it represents. But some couples stay married for religious reasons yet live with hate, abuse, or adultery instead of with love and trust. In such cases, is God's plan being followed?

If, like Ruth, you were the dumper and are feeling guilty because you had to end your marriage, pray about it. God understands. "If we confess our sins, he is faithful and just to forgive us our sins, and to cleanse us from all unrighteousness" (1 John 1:9).

Forgive yourself. God has.

SIX

Letting Go

Stage Four: Acceptance

Psychologists explain that sometime during the first year after a marriage ends, many of us progress to the fourth stage in the recovery process. In this stage we accept that the old life is over; we realize a new life is beginning.

As long as we stubbornly try to hold on to the old, we prevent the beginning of the new. As long as we continue to pound our heads against the wall, the hurting continues. It doesn't subside until we stop pounding and accept that we can't change what happened. Dwelling on it doesn't help.

Once we progress to the *acceptance stage*, we remember the past but it isn't the first thing we think about when we open our eyes each morning. We may even think, "I'm finished hurting, finally."

The days pass smoothly until suddenly, wham something happens. Maybe a certain song plays on the radio. Or you see your ex-husband with his new wife. Whatever it is, you slide backward and think you haven't made any progress at all.

But you have. Think back. In the beginning of the recovery process, every day was gloomy. Now during the times when you temporarily slip backward, you realize that before you slipped, life was beginning to be tolerable.

In the acceptance stage, you realize you're not as unhappy as you were in the early months after your marriage ended. You also know that, in a day or two, you'll feel better. I call the second year the zigzag year, because during this year your emotions seem to zig forward, zag backward, zig forward. . . .

Knowing this helped Carole get through the zag days following her divorce. "When Jim left," she said, "my whole world shattered. It was hard to let go. It was over a year before it dawned on me that bad days were coming less often and good days always followed."

Carole speaks for many divorcées. "When our marriages end," she said, "we mourn the ending of what *was*. Eventually, with time, we accept what *is*. Before we reach the acceptance stage, most of us fight long and hard against reality. But nothing changes.

"Eventually, we realize that the past is just that, past, over, gone, a memory. *Yesterday is no more.* After we finally accept what we have to, then, *surely*, we can believe that the worst is behind us. Can't we?"

Psychologists say that you can believe the worst is over only when you *completely* accept what *is*. When you get to this point, you will *know*. When you reach the acceptance stage, you understand that although you haven't completely recovered, you've come a *long* way. When you progress to this stage, you can accept that your marriage failed because something went wrong. It no longer seems important whether (like Ruth) you initiated the divorce or (like Carole) had it forced on you.

Most divorcées find this fourth stage, acceptance, the most difficult. Even though a judge officially ruled your marriage dissolved and denial has been worked through, traces of the past remain—particularly if children are involved. Graduations, weddings, and grandchildren are strong links to an ex-husband and the past. These links are like invisible bonds. They're tough to break. As you deal with these events, the bonds slowly unravel and fall away.

Acceptance is tough for widows, too. Many of us who were happily married tend to remember our husbands and marriages through a rosy haze. Psychologists call this rosy remembering "memorializing." They say that when memorializing occurs, our acceptance is hampered. How could anything so wonderful be over?

Some widows can't bring themselves to remove their husbands' clothing and personal things. They want to keep things the way they always were. Others remember only the goodness or kindness of their husbands' personalities. They forget the negatives of their marriages. Unintentionally, through memorializing, they elevate their husbands' memory to the status of near-sainthood.

I hate to admit it—but to some extent, I fell into the trap of memorializing. As the months following Ed's death slowly slithered by, the little aggravations that had occurred in our marriage began to fade. Instead of realistically remembering, I dwelled only on the happy times I remembered so well. When it dawned on me that I had slipped into memorializing, I shared my concern with Susan.

She nodded. "I know," she said. "After Ralph died, I memorialized too. It's an easy trap to fall into. But you can help yourself break out of it by making a list."

"A list?"

"Yes. First list all of Ed's good points. Write the things about him and your marriage that you love and miss."

"Okay," I agreed. "That's easy."

"After you make *that* list," she added, "then make a list of all the things about him and your marriage that you dislike."

That evening I chewed on my pencil, lost in remembering. Then I made my lists. As I wrote, my memories of the past became more realistic. Susan was right. My lists helped me to understand that my marriage was wonderful, but not perfect. Nothing this side of heaven is perfect.

Besides memorializing my husband and our marriage, removing my wedding ring on the first anniversary of Ed's death was a major milestone that helped me accept that our marriage was over. However, I still wear the eternity ring of twenty-five little diamonds that Ed gave me on our twenty-fifth anniversary the year before he died.

"Still memorializing?" Susan asked. She pointed to the eternity ring. "By continuing to wear that ring, aren't you subconsciously linking yourself to Ed?"

I thought about her question for days before concluding that my answer was *no*. I wear the ring because it's beautiful as well as symbolic of twenty-five years of my life. Twenty-five years is a big chunk, nearly half of my life, actually. Those years were good ones; I wear the ring to celebrate them. Wearing it has nothing to do with my accepting or not accepting Ed's death.

Susan shared other problems she had to deal with while trying to accept Ralph's death. "Before my acceptance was complete," she admitted, "the first year after Ralph died, I read everything on bereavement I could find. I wanted something, *anything* to help me accept his death."

I nodded.

"You'll think I'm crazy," she continued, "but I even talked to myself on a tape recorder. Later I would replay the tape and force myself to listen."

"Really? What did you tell yourself?"

"Stuff like 'Ralph is dead. Today is a new day. It isn't yesterday. It's a new day. One day at a time, I can do it. Tomorrow will be better.' "

She laughed and continued, "I suppose I sounded like a warped record with the needle stuck in a groove."

I smiled. "Do you think your little talks to your tape recorder helped?"

Susan shrugged her shoulders. "Who knows? I suppose so. At least they didn't hurt."

Whether divorced or widowed, the path leading to acceptance is rocky and treacherous. When we finally accept that reality can't be changed, the path becomes smoother. Then we pick up the pieces of our shattered world. Piece by piece, we put it together again.

SEVEN

Picking Up the Pieces

Stage Five: Recovery

Recovery. Isn't this a wonderful word? We reach the final stage in the recovery process when we initiate and follow through with plans to make our lives happy again. Most widows and divorcées I know say that recovery occurred sometime after the completion of the second year. I think this was true for me.

The first year is the toughest. We have to get through all the "first times." The holidays are especially painful. The hours creep. Many times we're sure we can't possibly cope with another day. But we do. The first anniversary of the death or divorce ends the most difficult year. The second year, the zigzag year, is a little easier. The pain is there but less intense. In the beginning there is no let up. The pain continues, day and night. Eventually we accept what we must and pack our memories away. We stop dwelling on the "if onlies" and "what might have beens."

If this sounds like you now, congratulate yourself. You've reached the *recovery stage!* In this stage you'll discover that being single again provides opportunities for new, interesting experiences. I once read that, to be happy, we need someone to love, something to do, and something to look forward to. Loving someone is easy. We love our children, relatives, and friends.

The second requirement is easy, too. There are many worthwhile things to do. We can donate spare time to favorite charities. We can attend church. We can develop interesting hobbies. We can return to school. We can learn new skills. There are hundreds of interesting and worthwhile things to do.

The last requirement, something to look forward to, needn't be difficult either. We must simply set realistic goals, then work toward achieving them. The goals can be as simple as losing ten pounds, or as complex as knitting a sweater. The important thing is to have a goal and to work toward achieving that goal.

There's one other thing we can do to make life more fulfilling. It involves *attitudes.* We can *change* attitudes. We can't control the future—but we can control our *attitudes* about the future. Think about it. If you continue frowning, your negative outlook will color your future. You can color the future gray or you can color it the many colors of the rainbow.

Remember, it takes rain *and* sunshine to make a rainbow. While coping with the end of my marriage and then working through the five stages of the recovery process, I've had my share of rain. I know you have, too. But look around. Sunshine surrounds you! Isn't it about time you reached for your rainbow?

EIGHT

Carrying on, Alone

Now that you're familiar with the five stages that psychologists tell us are part of the recovery process, you can understand that the way you feel today is normal. It is shared by other women starting over.

When starting over most of the problems divorcées and widows share are similar. But there is one major task only divorcées face. If you have children, you had to tell them that you and their father would no longer remain married. No doubt you dreaded telling them of this drastic change in your and their worlds.

No matter how hard you tried to hide your unhappiness from your children, they weren't fooled. They knew when tension existed between you and their father. They heard the arguing and the crying even if you thought they were sleeping. Don't fool yourself—kids aren't as unaware as you think.

When Carole told her two sons that their father wanted a divorce, they replied, "We're not surprised, Mom. But why? Why don't you and Dad love each other any more?"

"I had to bite my tongue," Carole answered. "I didn't want to tell the boys about Jim's girlfriend. I felt he should be the one to tell them."

"What did you tell them?" I asked.

She sighed. "I finally answered that their father and I no longer had the same priorities for our marriage. We weren't happy anymore. I know it was a cop-out," she continued, "but I just couldn't say the words. The boys would hear the hurt and bitterness in my voice."

I nodded. "When did Jim tell them the truth?"

"Two days after he moved out."

Your children may have been aware that there's un-happiness between you and their father. Even so, when you told them you were getting a divorce many probably had trouble accepting it. This is a normal re-action. Because their family unit is threatened, chil-dren sometimes fantasize that you and their father will work out the problems and change your minds. It's hard for them to give up the fantasy.

In his book, *Creative Divorce*, Mel Krantzler writes that the age of children at the time of their parents' di-vorce determines their reactions. Preschool children often regress to infantile behavior. Some revert to bed-wetting. After a parent moves from their home, some children cling to the parent and cry with every visit. This behavior may persist until the child realizes the absent parent won't disappear forever.

Unlike children, adolescents can understand that one parent will live in a different house. Adolescents fear the unknown and wonder whom they will live with. They worry whether they'll see both parents reg-ularly or have to move from friends.

Unfortunately, many children this age feel guilty when their parents no longer love each other. Some even believe the divorce is somehow their fault. Krantzler stresses this: Children must understand that their parents are divorcing *each other* and are not divorcing them. Children must not assume any responsibility for the divorce.

Teenagers often react with hostility when told parents are divorcing. As divorce proceedings progress, they sometimes vent their anger on the parent they live with. If a teenager sees a father only occasionally, for instance, he most likely won't direct his anger at the father. Instead, he'll probably release it at his mother, because in most cases he sees her every day.

Krantzler says that teenagers should be encouraged to express feelings. The more anxiety they express verbally, the less they will act it out. Even though your teenagers' feelings are often hostile, and you are usually the target for their anger, try to remain calm. It's difficult if a teenager is screaming that it's your fault his dad is leaving. But in the long run, the teenager's adjustment to the divorce will be easier if you remain calm.

Besides open hostility, some teenagers express their anger by refusing to talk to the parent they feel is responsible for their unhappiness. To get even, some rebel and refuse to do household chores. Others lose interest in school, and truancy becomes a problem.

Psychologists warn that along with denial, fear, and anger, most children also react to their parent's divorce with grief. Kids are sad because they won't see both their parents daily. And they're sad because they don't understand the complexities and unfairness of life.

How can you help your kids adjust to your divorce? Their father and you can assure your children that they are loved even though one of you no longer lives in the same house. You can explain that you know parting from someone they love is terribly painful and that, as parents, you also are both sad.

Some well-meaning parents feel they must make it up to their children because they no longer share a daily part of their kids' lives. Because they want to be *good* parents, they turn every visit into a fun outing. Others allow their children to stay up late at night. They believe responsibility for insisting that the kids clean their rooms, eat their vegetables, and finish their homework is left to the parent who sees them daily.

Don't let this happen to you and your children. Psychologists warn that if the more absent parents insist on this artificial relationship, they do their children more harm than good. Noncustody parents should maintain normal routines and discipline when with their children. Children are happier when confusion is avoided and they understand what is expected of them.

When your children return from visiting the other parent, don't let them manipulate you by whining, "But there we can leave our shoes in the living room. Why can't we do it here?" To avoid confusion for the kids, if possible, discuss expectations with your ex-spouse so the rules in each of the two homes are similar. The kids should understand that each house reflects the lifestyle of the parent who lives there.

When parents are at odds with each other, some

children turn *against* the absent parent while others become defensive on the absent parent's behalf. Because they love both parents, some children may feel guilty if they think they are betraying one of them. Psychologists caution that, if you are the parent with custody, you must *never* insinuate to your children that their other parent no longer loves them or doesn't have time for them. To do so is to feed insecurity which can persist throughout a child's life.

Some divorcées use their children as vehicles to cling to the past. Don't do this. Even though it's hard not to be curious after the kids have spent the weekend with their dad, don't pry by asking them personal questions about him. Your marriage is over, so it doesn't matter if your ex-husband has a woman friend or if he leaves dirty dishes stacked in the sink. He isn't your husband any more, so remind yourself that it's really none of your business.

When in contact with your ex-husband, keep the conversation short and impersonal and *never* use your children as weapons. Unless their father is destructive to your childrens' well-being, remember that he *is* their father and should be treated as such. The early years after the divorce are especially hard for the kids. Holidays are very difficult because they are reminders of happier times when the family was together. Now arrangements have to be made so that the children can spend the holidays with the absent parent as well as the custody parent.

Some couples solve this problem by rotating the holidays. For instance, the kids could spend Christmas with one parent this year and the other parent next year. Some parents want their children with them each holiday—if only for a few hours. Others celebrate the holidays on two separate days. It doesn't matter how you and their father work it out as long as your childrens' happiness is your main priority.

Psychologists tell divorcées and widows we shouldn't try to recapture the holidays by doing what we've always done. The holidays can't possibly be the same as they were in the past, so we shouldn't try to keep them the same.

Instead, we must make changes, start new traditions. For instance, you could put the Christmas tree in a different room this year. If you've always cooked the Thanksgiving turkey, ask someone else do it. Bake the pies instead. These are little but positive changes. Each positive change is a step forward.

While adjusting to being a single parent, not only do the holidays change, every day changes. There's just too much to do and the days aren't long enough, right? If you have a job and you've added more hours to your workday, your older children can help you by sharing some of the responsibilities. In some single-parent households, some older children may contribute financially. Some may help with the cooking, cleaning, and the care of younger brothers and sisters.

According to psychologists, added responsibility doesn't hurt children. When they help with responsibilities, many teenagers seem to mature overnight. Their self-esteem is boosted because they know they're needed and are respected for their contributions to the family's well-being.

If you're running around like a crazy woman, working full-time and trying to be two people, *stop. Think.* Ask yourself, "Am I being fair to myself and to my kids? Are my kids being fair to me?"

If the answer to these questions is "no," start making changes. Talk to your children. Explain that you aren't superwoman. Then for heaven's sake stop trying to act like her. I've discovered that when our kids understand that our lives have changed, most of them turn out to be pretty wonderful young people.

When Ed died, Tom, my oldest, was twenty-two. Mike, my middle son, was twenty. My youngest, Karen, was eighteen. After their father died, each in a special way began to help and encourage me. They still do. Tom helps me make financial decisions. Mike can repair anything. Karen provides company and hugs. They've matured into productive, self-sufficient, loving adults. I'm proud of them and I know Ed would be, too. I hope your children are also a blessing.

Besides relying on your children's help and understanding, you can help *yourself and them* by encouraging their relationship with their grandparents. Grandparents love their grandchildren and want their happiness as much as you do. Children thrive on love. Encourage the relationship between them and their grandparents—both yours and your ex-husband's parents.

If children have lived in a home where there's daily screaming matches, they should be exposed to homes where there is love and respect. If their grandparents love and respect each other, then by being around them the kids will see that marriage can be rewarding.

It's unfortunate when a father wants to remain a part

of his children's lives but he can't. Maybe he has moved to another state, or a second family takes most of his time. No one can take the place of a loving father in a two-parent home. If your children's father is not involved in their lives, it's important that positive male role models be provided for them. This is especially true if you have sons.

Male friends and relatives can substitute for an absent father. Volunteers from Big Brothers and boys' clubs sponsored by the church or community can provide opportunities for your sons to work and play around men and other boys.

Some churches are also helpful. In a Fort Lauderdale, Florida, church, the men have formed a Substitute Dad group. These men have organized group activities so that a core of men meet with children who are without fathers. The men take the kids to the beach, the zoo, picnics, skating, and Little League activities. They help the kids know God cares about them by showing them that God works through men that care. By providing Christian role models for children, these men touch the lives of young people who, through death or divorce, are robbed of their fathers.

I can't think of a better way Christ can be served than through these caring men. If your church doesn't have a Substitute Dad group, why not suggest that one be formed and do what you can to help get it going?

Death or divorce is devastating to children. Just as you are, your kids are going through a tough time. They have to make major adjustments, too. It's up to you to ensure that they are provided the emotional nourishment all children deserve.

NINE

Clinging to the End of Your Rope

Ruth shaded her eyes from the blazing summer sun. "Being single again after years of marriage is overwhelming," she said. "You know what I mean?"

I nodded and pulled my floppy hat farther down. At the beach, we were watching her son, Petey, build sand castles along the water's edge. As he patted wet sand into mounds, he looked up at his mother and smiled.

Ruth waved and said, "It's lonely and demanding. When I was a girl, divorce was rare. I only knew one girl whose parents were divorced. Back then raising children was shared by both parents. My dad's role was financial provider and disciplinarian. Mom took care of our house, bandaged skinned knees, and baked brownies. Yesterday's roles are outdated today," she sighed, "especially in a one-parent home like mine."

She unwrapped a peanut butter sandwich for Petey. "As bad as our marriage was," she continued, "I didn't want a divorce. I was afraid a divorced home wouldn't be good for Petey and Sharon. I couldn't face that the atmosphere in our home wasn't good for them either.

"So instead of leaving John, I pretended everything was fine. I pretended to myself, my parents and my friends. But then suddenly I was forced to stop pretending. There was no way I could pretend that my little boy's black eye and swollen face didn't exist."

She poured lemonade into a plastic cup and handed the cup and sandwich to her son. "I think one of the biggest changes in my life after the divorce was financial," she said. "Although John is an alcoholic, he did provide for us. Before my divorce, I worked part-time in a bank. Now I work full-time. We can no longer take for granted many things the kids and I used to assume we could have. There just isn't enough money."

Ruth's problem isn't unusual. Lack of money is a major problem for most single women. There's a big difference between working to add luxuries to the family's income and working to support the whole family. You may live on the salary you earn plus alimony and child support if you're divorced. Or you may live on your salary plus insurance benefits if you're widowed. But either way, the amount is usually far less than what you lived on before your marriage ended.

If you have children and your pay is inadequate, stretching the paycheck is a killer. If you have a job with substantial income, you can still sympathize with thousands of less fortunate single mothers. Some can't even depend on regular child support checks. In the United States, far too many fathers skip child support payments. Terrible, isn't it? Most delinquent fathers have remarried and started a new family. Money stretches just so far. Unfortunately, it seems children from first marriages are often neglected.

But it will soon be quite difficult for parents to skip support payments. In late 1988, Congress approved the first major revision of the welfare system in fifty-three years. By 1994, child support payments will automatically be deducted from every absent father's paycheck. Soon states will be required to obtain Social Security numbers of all parents. By 1994, child support deductions will be as automatic as Social Security deductions. This revision will benefit countless women who should, but don't, receive regular financial support for their children.

Another major problem many formerly marrieds face is loneliness. You probably have always lived with someone. First you lived with your childhood family. Then you married and lived with your husband's and your children. Now, for the first time in your life unless your children still live at home, you are alone.

If you are recently divorced or widowed, it's natural that you're lonely. I know you are because I was, too. But I discovered that unless I wanted to be, I didn't have to be lonely for the rest of my life. You don't either. There are millions of other single adults. Reach out to them. Although you aren't married any more, you can still enjoy the company of good friends.

Besides reduced income and loneliness, you face other burdens. You likely have a job that gobbles up eight to ten hours of the day. When you get home, you have to clean house, cook meals, do the laundry. You must do whatever chores your husband once handled. Whatever your roles once were, now you must buy car tires and cut the grass. You must paint the house and repair the garage door opener. You must unstop a plugged toilet or kitchen sink.

If you can afford it, you can pay someone to do these things for you. Otherwise you must do them yourself. Just thinking about them ties your stomach in knots. Now you have to do more than just think about them. They don't miraculously take care of themselves. You either have to do them or see that they get done.

I know many days you're so tired you can't think straight. You're sick of stretching your budget. You're tired of running to and from work, cleaning the house, and disciplining the kids. There are days you don't see how you can hang on much longer.

The temptation to give up is strong. After all, who really cares if the house is dusted or the laundry is folded? Who cares if you gain weight or don't bother with makeup anymore? Who notices?

The kids? Probably not. Does anyone really care? Yes. Who? *You.* At least I hope you do. When you're starting over you *must* care about yourself, otherwise you won't be able to make your life better. Start telling yourself over and over, "If my life is going to improve, it will be because I'm going to make it happen. No one will do it for me. *If it's to be, it's up to me!*"

Okay. Now, *how* are you going to go about it? To whom, or where, can you turn for help?

TEN

Getting Back on Your Feet

"Friends. They're worth their weight in gold. At least some of mine were during the first year after Ralph died," Susan said. "I don't know what I would have done without them. They were never too busy to listen to me those early months when I was self-absorbed with his death. They weren't embarrassed or annoyed when I cried, bellyached, or complained. They also helped when I needed an extra pair of hands. They continued to include me in their social activities."

I nodded. "I know what you mean," I said. "When Ed died, several of my close friends stuck by me, too. I really appreciate how supportive they were."

I held up my fingers and began to count. "Let's see, sometimes Ruby and Ed included me when they went out of town on weekends," I said, "and many times Cleo and Walt asked me to join them for dinner. Bev helped me make financial decisions and Ken built shelves in my new home.

"Then on the anniversaries of Ed's death," I continued, "in his memory, Micky and Marvin contributed to the American Cancer Society."

I smiled and held up my second hand and continued counting. "Molly and De listened and supplied Kleenex when I wallowed in self-pity. They're widows, too," I explained, "so they *understood* the way I felt.

"Also," I added, "Betty and Mary boosted my morale by sending 'thinking of you' cards. And Jean, Delores, Alice, Helen, and Jeanne called long-distance many times just to remind me that I was in their thoughts.

"Last but not least was my sister, Linda. She's a nurse; she nagged me with reminders that I had to continue eating to remain healthy for my kids' sake if not for my own. The love and friendship of these people helped me over many a rough hurdle."

When starting over, widows aren't the only ones who rely on close friends. Divorcées do, too. In the beginning, you had a difficult chore widows didn't share. You had to admit to your friends and relatives that your marriage was over.

Ruth nodded. "When we finally do tell our friends," she said, "we can't be too surprised if *they* aren't surprised. I guess it's impossible to hide unhappiness. Most of my close friends were aware that my marriage wasn't good. My news did surprise my acquaintances, though. Up until the divorce, I played the role of happily married wife and was good at pretending."

Carole was thoughtful. "Besides having to admit the ending of the marriage to friends," she said, "there's another problem divorcées have that widows don't share." She explained, "As news of the divorce spreads, many friends start to feel uncomfortable. If they're both your and your ex-husband's friends, they'll want to keep both friendships. They won't want to choose sides."

Carole and Ruth discovered that some friends tiptoed around their divorce. Other friends were curious and didn't hesitate to ask personal questions.

"A friend who had gone through a messy divorce advised me not to divulge too much," Carole said. "She told me that it would be better for my children if I kept the details private. I think she's right. Now I pass along her advice. I tell other divorcées that, if they feel they must provide explanations, they should tell their story briefly and eliminate most of the nitty-gritty."

Susan speaks for most of us when she says that, with the passing of time, a widening gulf sadly seems to separate our married friends from us.

"I never thought I'd say this," she admitted, "but as wonderful as they were after my marriage ended, most of my former friends and I have drifted apart over the years. I think this happened because my lifestyle changed and theirs didn't. My style of living, economically and socially, is light-years away from theirs now. We didn't deliberately plan this to happen, but it did."

She continued, "I think it happens because most married people are more comfortable with other marrieds. And single people tend to drift to other singles. This may be because married people don't realize that some of us feel uncomfortable standing around while they make plans with their husbands. It just doesn't occur to them that most of us hate feeling like a fifth wheel when everyone else is coupled."

"In all fairness," she added, "I don't think we can

blame our married friends. Unless they've been in our shoes, they really don't understand the changes in our lives. Besides, fifth wheels are an inconvenience. After all, what can they do with an extra woman at a dinner party? Or when several married couples usually meet Saturday evenings for dinner, how long can they continue to include the extra person?"

I nodded. "And when they do," I said, "there's the embarrassment of who pays the check."

"It's a real problem," Susan admitted. "The first time I tagged along to dinner with a married couple, it was comforting to sit back and let my friend's husband pick up the check. Men always do.

"But then when they invited me another time, I wanted to pay my share. My friend's husband wouldn't hear of it. I was too embarrassed to argue."

"I know," Carole said. "I always offer. But if a friend's husband insists on paying, I let him. Later I invite them both to dinner at my house."

While adjusting to being single again, you undoubtably have many gray days. I know because I did, and I'm sure you do, too. On these days you feel sorry for yourself and don't think you're fit company for anyone. When you're feeling gray, it's hard to reach out to friends. You imagine they're busy, so instead of calling someone you lock yourself into your gloom.

Psychologists tell us that while in these moods we can't sit around wishing life was more satisfying. We have to make the effort to meet new people as well as to remain in contact with old friends. We have to accept invitations and offer them. We have to develop different interests and talents and open our minds to new experiences. When we spend time with people we enjoy, doing things we enjoy, our days become more rewarding and less lonely.

While dealing with the changes in your life, organized support groups may be helpful in addition to friends. These groups meet weekly so members can provide and receive help from each other. These people know how rotten you feel because they've been, or still are, in the same shoes. When you share with others and they with you, you learn to laugh at yourself. While they're helping you, you're helping them.

A group formed specifically to provide social activities for its members is Parents Without Partners. This is a national organization with chapters located throughout the country. Members attend dances, plays, dinners, and concerts together. Look in the telephone book for the chapter in your area. Give them a call. You have nothing to lose and much to gain.

While you're adapting to starting over, professional counseling is also helpful. Most churches provide such services. If yours doesn't, ask your pastor for a referral or find a church that offers such help. When you discuss your problems with a counselor, one to one, you'll gain an objective insight into your thinking. Counselors aren't judgmental. As they listen, they'll provide feedback to help you deal with your feelings.

So if you need counseling, don't be afraid to seek professional help. And don't feel embarrassed at admitting you are floundering and need help to get on with your life. If you're worried about the expense, fees for church-supported counseling services are usually arranged on a sliding scale adjusted to your income. Discuss your finances with your church's director, and a suitable schedule of fees can be agreed on.

You're the one starting over. Although your friends, old and new, want to help you, the *effort* must be *yours*. You owe it to yourself to do all that you can to make your life interesting and satisfying again. For many widows and divorcées, joining a support group or getting professional counseling is exactly what is needed to boost progress.

As we struggle through the ups and downs of starting over, I think God helps us, too. How? I believe God is in the love and caring of good friends. He's in our churches and support groups. He's in the knowledge of professional counselors. He listens to our prayers. So while you're getting back on your feet, don't delay in asking for help. Pick up the telephone. Help may be just a call away.

ELEVEN

Keep the Welcome Mat Out

"When marriage ends, formerly marrieds should find emotional support in their church, right?" Ruth asked. "Why, then," she continued, "instead of serenity and acceptance, do most of us feel alienation and discomfort?"

Carole thought for several minutes before she answered. "I think," she said, "the answer is that churches are traditionally geared for families.

"With over 12 million widowed and divorced in this country, you'd think churches would realize not every family has a husband and a wife. Many times activities in the womens' classes at my church suggest that we bring our husband.

"But what about those of us who no longer have a husband to bring? Sure, I can come alone but I feel like I have four arms and two heads. I feel *different*. I wish people in the church would realize that an emphasis on family events is uncomfortable for those of us who no longer have a complete family."

Susan agrees. "In my church the sermons and Sunday school discussions are often directed to the problems of the married. Because of this I've felt out of place many times. I never dreamed when my husband was alive that there'd be times I'd feel uncomfortable in God's house." She sighed and continued, "After Ralph died it was almost as if the church yanked away the welcome mat."

Carole nodded. "It's too bad that many divorcées and widows feel uncomfortable in church. Discomfort alienates and separates. Since households headed by single people are increasing, churches should realize that a lot of us in the congregation aren't married anymore. I don't think it dawns on the other members that singles often feel their needs are lost in the shuffle of the family atmosphere."

"Carole's right," Susan added. "Caring churches should try to meet the needs of *all* members, regardless of marital status. Can you think of ways you wish your church would change its focus to include our needs, Carole?"

"Can I!" Carole exclaimed. "Just listen. The adult Sunday school classes are geared either for young singles or married couples. Where does that leave me? I'm not 'young' anymore so I certainly don't belong in a *young* single's class.

"Sure I'm single," she went on, "but I don't fit in with the college-age singles either. So where do I belong? With the married couples? Not likely. It's easy to see why the divorced and widowed drift away from Sunday school. Churches need to provide Sunday school classes for older singles."

Ruth listened quietly. "As long as we're offering suggestions," she said, "I'd like to see churches serving as substitute families for those of us with severed families. Unfortunately," she sighed, "this isn't the case. At least in my church it isn't.

"I also think that the problems of widows and divorcées are skipped over in church sermons. If an occasional focusing on our problems was included, maybe we'd feel more welcome."

Ruth nodded her agreement. "I don't think church dinners should be called 'Family Nights' either," she said. "For most of us, the word 'family' brings to mind a mother, a father, and children. It would be kinder to have 'Friendship Nights' instead. The name is more friendly and certainly more welcoming."

"And, how about occasional weekend retreats combined with other churches of the same denomination?" Carole suggested. "If several churches combined retreats, then a wonderful opportunity to meet new Christian people could be provided."

"Since churches are usually geared for families, many of us don't feel comfortable sitting alone in a church pew," Ruth added. "If members understood that some of us are sensitive about our aloneness, they could try to be more friendly. At one time or another, we're all guilty of rushing in to or out of church without acknowledging the people around us.

"Sure, we nod and smile," she said, "but we're in such a hurry, we don't take the time to *see* each others' needs. This is unfortunate, because when we're feeling hurt and lonely a friendly word is so helpful."

"There's something else we haven't mentioned," Susan added. Carole, Ruth, and I looked at her expectantly. "I think it's easy enough to be critical," she said, "but part of the problem is our fault. We need to keep our sensitivities in check.

"For instance," she continued, "if the pastor of our church isn't as emotionally supportive as we wish, we should realize he has hundreds of members in the congregation. His time is limited. My pastor visited me once after Ralph died. I realize he probably didn't have time for a follow-up visit. I think he felt that if I needed him again, I'd let him know."

"Mmmmm," Carole said. "At least he visited. When Jim left and the news of our divorce spread throughout my church, my pastor didn't call to see if there was anything he could do."

"Mine didn't either," Ruth added. "I guess the *way* a marriage ends must make a difference. Don't pastors realize that members who are newly divorced need to be added to their visitation list? I wish my pastor had thought it important to visit and pray with me sometime during the first few months after my divorce."

We agreed that even though we wish churches were more supportive of the widowed and divorced, we shouldn't be too judgmental. Until people experience the ending of their marriages, it's impossible *really* to understand.

Susan summed up our feelings. "Think about it," she said. "Either divorce or death ends all marriages eventually. Someday each married person in the church will walk in our shoes. Then perhaps he or she will understand."

When this happens, we believe God expects the divorced and the widowed to help them. Because we'll truly understand, we can then emulate Christ's teaching and be compassionate and caring. "In the church God has put all in place . . . to help others. . . ." (1 Cor. 12:28, GNB).

If we wish our churches were more emotionally supportive, we can try not to give in to disappointment. The church is a place to worship and join in fellowship with others who love our Lord. Even if we are sometimes uncomfortable and feel left out, we can continue to attend church and participate in its activities. We can let members know the needs of the formerly married and make suggestions for possible alternatives.

God already understands our needs, but we can pray for the understanding of the members in our congregation. With our efforts and their understanding, perhaps God's house will once again be the refuge for all of us that God means it to be.

TWELVE

Opening New Doors

"Wow, what a rude awakening," Carole said. "After months of curling up on the couch in front of the TV, I finally realized I have to stop procrastinating and make an effort to meet other men. But after twenty-two years of marriage, I don't know how to begin."

"Carole," I said, "how about your friends? Do any of them know a single man they can introduce you to? What about your job? Any interesting men there?"

She shook her head. "Not really. Everyone I work with is married. Or too young. Or too something. Where are all the decent single men, anyway?"

"There's one thing certain," Susan chimed in. "They aren't in your family room. You won't meet anyone sitting in front of your television night after night. I think your best bet is through an activity you like. Most likely a man you'll meet there enjoys that activity, too."

"How about classes at the university?" I suggested.

"Or hobbies men are interested in?" Ruth added.

Carole sighed. "My hobby is gourmet cooking. I'm always experimenting with new recipes. Jim and I used to go to a different gourmet restaurant every Saturday night. I loved to sample the different cuisines.

"But after the divorce," she added, "my friends told me they saw Jim and his girlfriend in one of our favorite restaurants."

Carole made a face. "Even if a man does invite me out," she said, "I certainly don't want to run into *them* there."

"Meeting a decent man or running into your ex-husband aren't the only problems," Susan said. "I have a single friend whose children don't want her to date."

"Really? Why is that?" Carole asked.

"I'm not sure. Maybe it's because when she dates someone, it forces her kids to accept that she and their dad aren't going to get back together. Some kids find this hard to handle."

Carole nodded. "Your explanation makes sense. How does your friend handle the problem?"

"At first it was tough," Susan answered. "Every time she introduced a new man to her teenage daughter, her daughter picked him apart. 'What do you see in him?,' she'd say. 'He's not as nice as Dad, nor as good looking. He's a zero, Mom.' "

Carole flinched. "Oh, that's mean. How did your friend deal with that?"

"She knew she had to be firm. She told her daughter that it takes time to get to know someone, and she wished the daughter would stop making snap judgments. She explained that she was trying to rebuild her life. She wanted her daughter to understand how difficult starting over is, especially for middle-aged women who don't look like Sophia Loren."

We laughed. "Right on," Carole said. "But did it do any good? Was there a change in her daughter's attitude?"

"Yes, eventually. At least now she tries to understand her mother's situation."

We were at a shopping mall. Carole, Ruth, Susan and I had stopped at a little pastry shop for refreshment. As Carole stirred cream into her second cup of coffee she looked up and said, "I think the cliché about "merry widows" and "happy divorcées" is a crummy myth. There's nothing merry or happy about either. Being single isn't exactly a bag of laughs, and Robert Redford isn't ringing my phone."

Susan laughed out loud. "I hope you aren't holding your breath waiting for his call," she said. "Dating is different now from when we were in high school. At least then the ratio of boys to girls was about even. It's a far cry from that at our age. Did you know that single women in their forties and fifties far outnumber single men in the same age group? And that's not all," she added. "The older we get, the more our numbers increase and theirs decrease."

"It's true men don't have a problem finding a woman to date," Ruth said. "There are so few of them and lots and lots of us." She sighed, "They really have it made, don't they? They can be as selective as they wish. I wonder," she added, "who do you think they most prefer to date, widows or divorcées?"

"That's a good question," Susan said. "Let's find out."

Carole giggled. "And just how do you suggest we do that?"

"Well," Susan answered, "we could ask the few middle-age single men we know."

So the following week, we did.

The first man I questioned was divorced. He admitted he'd rather date divorcées than widows. When I asked why, he replied, "Divorcées try harder to be congenial and many of them seem to need to prove to themselves that they're still desirable.

"On the other hand," he continued, "most widows don't care about proving anything and tend to expect more."

The second man was also divorced. "Given a choice," he said, "I'd date a divorcée. A widow makes it difficult to compete with her deceased husband. I don't like having to compete with a 'virtuous ghost.' On the other hand," he noted, "a divorcée tends to compare her ex-husband to a toad with warts. That certainly tips the scales in my favor."

My curiosity was aroused. I wondered if widowers have similar preferences regarding the women they date.

The first widower I questioned said, "I'd rather date widows because they usually have good memories of their marriages. They don't spend the evening complaining about their ex-husbands.

"When your marriage ends by fate, not fault," he went on, "it's hard to relate to a lot of the marital problems the divorced had. I can't help but wonder why something couldn't have been done to save their marriages. Maybe they just didn't try hard enough."

The second widower agreed with the first. "I prefer to date a widow," he said. "We understand each other's memories. I'm not threatened by her memories because I have my own. There's never a reason for me to be jealous of her 'ghost spouse' because I have one, too."

After listening to these four men, I concluded that when a divorced man dates a divorcée, his ego isn't threatened. He figures that, in her eyes, his past competition was a loser. His confidence is also boosted because he knows that if her marriage wasn't happy, she'll probably see him as a better man than her ex-husband.

The widowers, on the other hand, tended to experience marriages that, for the most part, were satisfying. That may be why they seem to relate more easily to widows. Their marriages, as well as the endings, were similar.

My little survey was far from scientific, but I thought the results were interesting. I shared my findings with Carole, Ruth, and Susan a few days later.

"I'm not surprised," Ruth said. "The responses of those men make sense. Although I do think it's a little silly for formerly married men to limit their dating experiences like that."

Carole nodded her agreement. "But don't forget about the ratio," she reminded us. "Men can afford to be choosy. Those men probably date both widows *and* divorcées, though. You asked them their *preference*, not *whom* they date."

"While I was snug in my married world, the singles scene was a light year away," Susan said. "I never gave it a thought. Now that I'm a part of it, I feel like Rip Van Winkle; I've awakened on an alien planet. All the rules

I remember from my dating days have changed."

She sighed, "Practically *everything* I remember about dating is obsolete. Remember in our day," she said, "only men did the inviting and the paying? No more. Due to the shortage of men, it isn't unusual for women to do the inviting as well as picking up the evening's tab."

"It's probably because most single men in our age group are still paying child support, college tuition, or alimony," Ruth said. "Although I think most of them still are more comfortable when they do the paying, they can't always afford to. To help out, some of the women I know occasionally buy tickets to concerts and athletic events or they fix home-cooked meals for their dates. There's nothing wrong with that. Maybe it was time for some of the rules about who pays what on dates to change."

Many divorcées and widows decide not to open the door to the dating scene again. Perhaps this is because many of the traditional dating rules have disappeared, or due to the lack of available, middle-age single men. Sometimes their age is a factor.

But for those of us who do date, stepping into the singles' dating circle is a new, unique experience.

THIRTEEN

Second Time Around?

Let's assume that you've met a man and you've dated him long enough to wonder if maybe, just maybe, he might be your Mr. Right. You no longer believe in fairy tales as you did when a young bride. You're an independent adult woman now. Perhaps you have children. Certainly you have responsibilities, prior attitudes, habits, and emotional baggage. Are you open to the possibility of walking down the aisle again?

Many formerly marrieds admit to being hesitant about making a second commitment. Starting over is stressful. Learning to be independent wasn't easy. But you did it and you're proud of your accomplishment. Most of you even discovered you like being independent. The longer you remain single, the more difficult it is to relinquish that independence.

Carole speaks for most of us. "I'm used to doing what I want to do when I want to," she said. "If I want to eat popcorn in bed, I do. If I don't feel like cooking a meal, I don't. Marrying again would be a *big* adjustment.

"I doubt that I could ever be a dependent wife again. I've changed too much. Now that my children are grown, the time for putting my needs on hold is past. For me to marry again, there would have to be a clear understanding of what my role as a wife would be."

Ruth nodded in agreement. "If I remarry, I expect a husband to provide emotional support and companionship. I starved for that when I was married to John."

She smiled and continued, "I know 'cherish' is an old fashioned word, but I'd want to be cherished and to cherish the man I married. I'd want each of us to be the other's best friend. Does that sound silly?"

"Absolutely not," Susan said. "Ralph and I had that. Never settle for less. But although we had a good marriage," she continued, "if I marry again, there are a few things I'd want to change."

"Really?" I asked. "What things?"

"Financial equality, for one. After six years of being single again, I've gotten used to spending money without having to ask anyone's permission. I know I'd want an equal voice in the way my new husband and I spent our money. Ralph always controlled our finances. I wouldn't want that again."

She paused. "By the way," she said, "are you aware that as long as we don't remarry, widows can collect their husband's social security at a reduced rate at age sixty? And if divorcées were married ten years, they can, too."

We nodded. "You know what worries me?" Susan added. "If any of us remarry before age sixty and the marriage doesn't work out, we'll forfeit our first husband's social security. And unless we're married ten years, we aren't entitled to the second husband's. To me, that's scary."

Giving up your independence and your right to an ex-husband's social security benefits aren't the only problems to consider if you're thinking of getting married again. Have you thought about whose house you will live in—yours or his? Or will you sell both houses, combine the money, and buy another house? How will you handle the checking and savings accounts? Combine them or keep them separate? What about the bills? Combine them or each pay his own?

If you have children and they still live with you, their attitudes regarding your remarriage could present a lot of problems. Do they like your Mr. Right? Can they accept him as their stepfather? And if your prospective husband has children, are you prepared to be their stepmother? Unfortunately, statistics show that many second marriages are sabotaged by children, his or yours. The demands of children and stepchildren can, and often do, present major problems in a second marriage. And don't forget, besides the two sets of children to be merged, there are former in-laws, ex-spouses, and a parcel of relatives to consider.

Besides successfully merging two families, both partners in a fulfilling second marriage must be willing to blend habits and expectations. This is easier said than done. Old expectations die hard. One partner can't remain rigid and insist that the other do all the bending. It won't work, at least not for long.

If each partner isn't willing to make the effort, a divorce could follow closely behind the second marriage. Statistics show that when divorced people remarry, their divorce rate is twice that in the first marriage. The rate increases with each remarriage and redivorce.

Now that you've considered negative possibilities of remarrying, let's think about the positives. It's wonderful to live harmoniously with the man with whom you want to share your world. When there is consideration for each other's feelings and each of you treat the other with respect and kindness, a closeness cocoons the two of you as you share the "for better or for worse" times in your lives.

Many years ago I read a beautiful definition of a good marriage. I wish I could remember where I read it. It was "a good marriage has the four c's: communication, caring, cuddling, and commitment." I think this definition is perfect, don't you? Over four hundred years ago Martin Luther wrote, "There is no more lovely, friendly and charming relationship, communication or company than that of a good marriage." He couldn't have said it better.

Is there a way to know for certain that a second marriage would be like this? Can we ever be *sure*? Not really. Marriage doesn't come with a happiness guarantee. A good marriage takes a lot of effort; it doesn't just happen. Marriage counselors tell us that second time arounders aren't kids anymore so our expectations are more realistic. They say that if we aren't mistaking the end of loneliness for love, if we aren't grasping for security, if we have a similar value system and sense of commitment with our Mr. Right, then chances are good that a second marriage will be successful.

Some formerly marrieds decide they like being single and choose to remain single for the rest of their lives. Some remain single because they never find the right person. Then there are those who don't find the right person but remarry anyway. And, of course, there are the few fortunate ones who find the right person and do remarry.

How does the Christian church view remarriage for us? Is a second chance for happiness permitted? The Scriptures provide answers but because interpretations are varied, many people believe that God's Word on remarriage is confusing. Just what does Scripture say?

"The Lord God said, 'It is not good that the man should be alone; I will make him an help meet for him" (Gen. 2:18). So far so good. Each of us found our "help mate" and married him. Like every bride on her wedding day, each of us believed marriage was permanent. But, it didn't turn out that way. We are single again. Now what? Is it okay to marry a second "help mate"?

Susan asked the pastor of her church to help with clarification. He explained that when a husband dies, a widow is free to remarry. "If her husband be dead, she is free from that law; so that she is no adulteress, though she be married to another man" (Rom. 7:3).

Okay, fine. But what about a divorcée? How does God feel about remarriage for you?

"Many Christian churches discourage remarriage for the divorced," Susan's pastor explained.

Scripture does say, "Whosoever shall put away his wife, and marry another, committeth adultery against her. And if a woman shall put away her husband, and be married to another, she committeth adultery" (Mark 10:11-12).

"However," the pastor continued, "in most Protestant churches, permission to remarry is granted when the divorce occurred *before* Christ was accepted."

Scripture says, "When anyone is joined to Christ, he is a new being; the old is gone, the new has come" (2 Cor. 5:17, GNB).

Some Christian denominations have a more tolerant approach to remarriage for the divorced. Their thinking is explained by Dr. Charles Allen in his book, *When a Marriage Ends.* He suggests that "until death do us part" is not limited only to the physical body but may also mean that love can die, too. He emphasizes the importance of forgiveness by reminding us that God forgives his followers.

"If God forgives our sins when we pray for forgiveness," Dr. Allen writes, "then why wouldn't he forgive our sin for being in a marriage that did not work out? Why wouldn't he forgive our part in it and grant us a second chance for happiness? Although God approves of marriage and not of divorce, he forgives us and his grace permits his children the opportunity for a new beginning."

Second time around for you? Whether to say "I do" again is a thought-provoking question. Through prayer, let God's guidance determine your answer. Only then can you be sure your decision is the right one.

FOURTEEN

The Metamorphosis

"If Ralph could see me now," Susan said, "he'd be surprised. He'd never believe how much I've grown."

"Sure, you've regained all the weight you lost during the months he was sick," Ruth teased.

"Come on, Ruth, that's *not* what I mean."

"I know. I just couldn't resist."

Susan smiled and pushed the plate of chocolate cake from her place. "You're right, of course," she sighed, "but I was thinking of other ways."

"What ways?"

"To begin with, I'm more relaxed about unimportant things. When I was married, little things really bothered me. I used to get annoyed more quickly than I do now. Now I just shrug the annoyances off. They aren't worth getting upset over. My whole attitude is different."

Carole nodded. "I know what you mean because I've changed, too. I was a good wife, I know I was. When Jim dumped me, it was awful. You see, I always depended on him for everything. I never bought a dress unless he liked it. His approval meant everything to me."

She ran her fingers through short auburn hair. "I never even cut my hair because Jim liked it long. As you can see, I wear it the way *I* like it now.

"I had a lot of growing up to do," Carole continued. At first I was scared. But once I learned I could pay my bills and make major decisions alone, I was elated. The responsibilities were overwhelming at first, but I love the feeling I have when I prove to myself I can accomplish almost everything I put my mind to. I'll *never* be completely dependent on anyone again."

"I agree," Ruth said. "The night I left John, I knew I had to be responsible for myself and the kids. I was scared. Now I know that when I handle each decision, each obstacle alone, I gain self-confidence."

She smiled. "You know," she went on, "we build layers of confidence similar to the way Petey builds with toy blocks—slowly, one block or step at a time. Then as our confidence grows, without being aware of it, we become stronger, more independent."

As Carole, Susan, and I murmured agreement, Ruth wiped her hands, then said, "When John was drinking, I couldn't depend on him, so I haven't changed much in that way. The biggest change divorce brought to my life was peace. I'm no longer on pins and needles wondering if John will be sober when he walks through the door. I'm so much more relaxed now. I haven't had a headache in months."

Single again in mid-life, each of my friends changed from the woman she was before her marriage ended. Now Susan keeps life's little annoyances in perspective. Carole is self-reliant. Ruth enjoys peace of mind. Although we teased Susan that her "growth" is the result of cupcake binges, we knew better. When formerly marrieds adapt to being single again, growth far exceeds the few pounds gained from overindulgence in sweets.

After I left my friends that afternoon, I thought about our conversation. The term *growth* danced through my mind. In the seven years since Ed died, I know I've grown a lot, too.

When he was alive, I was a dependent wife. Ed was an honest, reliable man, so I rarely worried about anything. My days revolved around him and our three children. I took pride in seeing that my household ran smoothly.

I tried to copy Harriet Nelson and Margaret Anderson. They were perfect wives and mothers on '50s and '60s TV shows. These ladies presided over spotless, make-believe homes. They *always* looked lovely and *never* lost their tempers. Although it was impossible to be like them, I tried. My kids called me their "Kool-Aid Mom" because I spent hours passing out Kool-Aid and homemade cookies to them and their friends. I played the "perfect wife and mother" role and filled it well.

When Ed died suddenly, I was lost. Not only did I lose the person in the world dearest to me, I lost a big hunk of my identity. Dazed, I muddled through the days, miserable and lonely. A friend's teenage son was killed in an automobile accident the year before Ed died. She told me that writing in a journal helped her to work through her grief.

I was desperate to try anything to ease my sorrow.

So, following her advice, I started scribbling my feelings of anger, guilt, and loneliness into a notebook. Some days I wrote for hours; other days I didn't write at all. As the months slowly passed, the little notebook grew. Eventually I tucked it away.

I also exchanged my part-time job as a substitute teacher for a full-time job teaching in a high school. The following year, I enrolled in a university. In night classes I began piling up credits toward a master's degree in English.

One class assignment was to write about the most difficult period of my life and the changes brought by the experience. No need to think twice. I pulled out the notebook I had tucked into a desk drawer, rewrote parts of it, and turned in the assignment. After the project was graded, I returned it and the notebook to the desk drawer.

The following year, a friend's husband died. I *knew* how she felt. I wanted to help her, but how? Somehow I had to let her know that she wouldn't always feel as hopeless as she did then. To help her and other widows, I dug into my desk and found the notebook and English project. For months I hunched over my old portable typewriter, fingers flying across the keyboard. When I finished, I crossed my fingers and dropped the manuscript into the mailbox.

Until Death Do Us Part was born.

Without my faith and help from God, I know I could not have written a book. I'm sure God leaned over my shoulder night after night as I typed, scratched out, and retyped. Most of my attempts were wadded and thrown into the overflowing trash can. But then I'd start over, again and again.

After writing *Until Death Do Us Part*, I learned that the ending of marriage is traumatic, not only for widows, but for divorcees, too. The ending of marriage, whether through death or through divorce, is traumatic—period. I have several friends who are divorced. Because they told me they experienced many of the problems I did when I had to start over, I wrote *Starting Over* with them in mind. I hope that while you are beginning again, this book will provide encouragement for you.

Carole asked if I would have attempted writing if Ed hadn't died. I doubt it. I think that when a marriage ends, a part of us dies. To live again, we have to develop a part of ourself that is underdeveloped. I believe each of us has a special talent, and God expects us to develop that talent in God's name.

How can you develop your special talent? Can you know God's will for you? The Bible provides the answer: "In all thy ways acknowledge him, and he shall direct thy paths" (Prov. 3:6).

I figured that if God promised to direct my path, what better guide could I possibly have than God? I talked to myself. "Okay, Self," I said. "If God promises to help you, what will it take to make you happy again?"

"That's easy," I answered. "I want to return to yesteryear when Ed was alive and my world was snug."

"That's impossible. It's a little girl's wish."

"I suppose it is," I admitted.

"Okay, Self," I continued, "I'll be adult. What do I want to do with the rest of my life? What does God want me to do? Does he have plans for me?"

"He must. He says he does: 'I know the plans I have for you . . . plans . . . to give you a future and a hope' " (Jer. 29:11, RSV).

I closed my eyes and whispered, "Please God, help me. What are your plans for me? What do you want me to do?"

I think we have to give God a chance to work in our lives. Each needs to develop the unique gift God gives. As the apostle Paul said, we have to tell ourselves, "I can do all things through Christ which strengtheneth me" (Phil. 4:13).

Because our lives changed, Carole, Ruth, Susan, and I changed. This is true for all divorcées and widows I know. When each of us accepted that our life was no longer going to be the same as before marriage ended, it finally sunk in that the key to happiness is *change*. Then a metamorphosis took place.

First, of course, we had to work through the five stages of the recovery process. There were no short cuts. But then, like the phoenix, the legendary bird in Egyptian mythology, Carole, Ruth, Susan, and I also rose from ashes. When we emerged, we became different, stronger women. We struggled through life's most stressful trauma, learned from it, and grew.

So can you.

FIFTEEN

Beginnings: Moving Forward!

Carole

Carole surveyed the tiffany lamp she held in her hands. She admired its beauty and intricate pattern of colors. She loved the lamp and never tired of looking at it. It had been in her family as long as she could remember. Carole first became mesmerized by it when she was a little girl visiting her grandmother.

Understanding Carole's love for the lamp, her grandmother gave it to her, just before she died. Because it had belonged to her grandmother and because of its fragile loveliness, the lamp was Carole's most treasured possession.

The pale sun darted behind clouds as spring rain splattered against the windows. Carole returned the lamp to its place and pulled the slender chain. Instantly the room was illuminated with warmth and light.

Carole poured a cup of coffee and settled into an easy chair. She tucked one foot beneath her and glanced around the room. The house was spotless. She wanted everything to be perfect. Jim was coming tonight for her answer.

Lost in thought, Carole sipped her coffee. She had dreamed about this day for a long time. The dream kept her going, helped her cling to sanity throughout the dismal first two years following the divorce. In those years her mind had pictured today at least a thousand times. Each time she had imagined it in a different way. But the outcome would always be the same: First Jim would admit his mistake. Then he'd beg her to forgive him. The dream always ended with their remarriage.

Life is ironic. As the years slipped by Carole finally gave up the dream. Now that it no longer mattered, the dream could become a reality. Just like that. Amazing. All she had to do was say, "Yes."

But did she want to? Did she still love Jim? Carole was no longer sure.

She had fallen in love with Jim when they were in high school. They married shortly after graduation. Throughout their marriage, his happiness was always her first priority. When he told her he was no longer in love with her and loved a young secretary in his office, Carole's world shattered into a hundred pieces.

For a while during the early months after the divorce, Carole thought she couldn't make it through each day. But she did. Eventually she learned to pick up the pieces of her world. Very slowly she put them back together. Five years is a long time. Jim was no longer the light of her life. She had adjusted to life without him.

Now Jim wanted to reenter her life. Should she let him?

The afternoon shower diminished; the sun slid from behind the clouds. Carole took her empty cup to the kitchen, rinsed it, and set it on the counter. Then she returned to the living room to switch off the little lamp.

Suddenly, everything seemed amazingly clear. The lamp, her *special* lamp, contained a message for her. Why hadn't she understood it before?

Her fingers lovingly traced the smooth surface. The shade wasn't really *whole*. It was composed of many, many tiny pieces of colored glass. Each piece was placed adjacent to the other. Where the pieces didn't fit together perfectly, glue supported and held them securely. The separateness of each tiny piece contributed to the loveliness of the entirety. If the lamp's shade were a solid substance, it would not be nearly as unique nor as lovely.

Carole's marriage had shattered. Could it, like the lamp, be pieced together a little at a time to become whole and lovely again? This time, with the right "glue," could the marriage endure and "shine" with love?

Carole smiled. Jim said he had changed. Well, she had changed, too. Jim said he loved her and wanted to put the pieces of their marriage together again.

Could remarriage be possible? Perhaps. And perhaps not. But "date" each other? A little smile played at the corner of Carole's lips. Date? Why not? Who knows, with time, maybe, just maybe. . . .

Ruth

As she applied makeup, Ruth smiled at her reflection in the mirror. "How do I look, Joyce?" she asked. Then she spun around. "Do you like my dress?"

I laughed. "You look beautiful, Ruth. It's wonderful to see you this happy."

"I *am* happy," she agreed. "And I feel marvelous!"

I hugged her. "Stand still so I can pin this corsage to your dress."

She obeyed. "I think I'm the luckiest woman in the world, I really do. Mark is a wonderful man," she said. "He's good with Petey, and Sharon likes him, too. Right, Sherrie?"

"He'll pass, Mom. Yeah," Sharon teased. Then she added, "I suppose you should keep him." Perched on the end of her mother's bed, Sharon was applying pale pink polish to her nails. She held her hands in front of her lips and blew on her nails to speed the drying.

"Are you nervous, Mom? After all, it's not every day you get married."

Ruth sat beside her daughter. "Nervous? Yes, I suppose I am," she admitted. "I never thought I'd want to marry again. After your dad and I divorced, getting married again was the last thing on my mind."

Ruth walked to the window and her eyes were misty. Her voice softened. "I loved John for a long time," she said. "Since high school days, really. He loved me, too. But over the years, his love changed. Alcohol stole it from me. Eventually I realized I could never win against my rival. I had to give up."

I patted her hand. "Maybe someday John will accept the help he needs."

She nodded. "I hope so. I prayed for that for years. I used to beg God to help John and our marriage. But it wasn't meant to be. I had to accept it.

"Life's funny, isn't it? Who would have thought I'd meet someone to love again? Who would have believed a man as special as Mark would love me, too?"

"I'm not surprised," I answered. "You're a special lady. Mark sees that."

She turned from the window and smiled. "God granted me a second chance for happiness when he sent Mark into my life. He's a pastoral counselor, you know. He understood the guilt I felt after I left John. He helped me to realize I had to stop punishing myself because John wouldn't stop drinking."

"Does John know you're remarrying?" I asked. "Have you told him?"

"Yes, of course. He didn't have much to say other than to wish me happiness. He's been sober for three months this time. He seems to want to get his life together. At least now he's admitting that he's an alcoholic. Mark says this is a positive step."

"I wish him the best," Ruth continued. "I always did. I was confused and unhappy for a long time after our divorce. I'm so thankful the pastor of my church suggested I attend group therapy. If he hadn't, I might never have forgiven myself for divorcing John. I wouldn't have met Mark, either."

"And today wouldn't be your wedding day," I added. "Your sister and Petey are probably at the church by now. Are you ready? We should leave soon."

She put her arm around her daughter's shoulders.

"I'm ready. How's my maid of honor's fingernails? Are they dry?"

"You bet, Mom."

"Then let's go. We have a wedding to go to! Mark and our guests are waiting. He and I have a lot of happiness to catch up on."

"Mom?"

"Yes, Sherrie?"

"You look terrific!"

As they hugged each other, I smiled and closed the door behind them.

Susan

Susan sat on a wooden box and looked around her living room. It was nearly bare. The movers would arrive soon. They would put the few pieces of remaining furniture and assorted cartons into the van. It was too late for second thoughts.

Susan bit her lower lip. "It's going to be all right," she told herself, "It's going to be all right."

The new apartment, clean and spacious, was waiting. She thought about the ways she would arrange the furniture. There wasn't a whole lot to arrange. To cut down the moving expense, she had sold most of it. She knew she wouldn't need it. She rented her house to a young couple, friends of friends. They'd move in next week.

For months she had anticipated and planned for this day. Now it was here. This afternoon she and her daughter, Laura, would close the door for the last time, say their good-byes, and be on their way.

It was exciting to think about the new job she'd have

teaching at the college. It would be challenging and, she hoped, fulfilling. There would be so much to do—learning her way around the new city, meeting new people, making new memories.

Her decision to uproot wasn't impulsive. Impulsive isn't Susan's style. Born in Miami, she had lived in the same house since she and Ralph bought it twenty years before. At that time the house was more expensive than they could afford, but they bought it anyway. They couldn't help it, they loved it from the instant they opened the double doors and stepped inside. The owners, an elderly couple, were eager to sell. Because it needed repair, the price was negotiable.

Over the years Susan and Ralph remodeled, planted shrubbery, and turned the house into their home. Susan loved to sit on her back porch and look down the grassy slope to the lake. She loved the family barbecues under the shade of the golden shower tree on lazy summer afternoons.

She loved the white adobe brick fireplace, too. Ralph had built it when the kids were little so they'd have a place to hang their stockings on Christmas Eve. Of course it wasn't a real fireplace. That would have been ridiculous in southern Florida, where the temperature hovers near 72 degrees all winter. Although it wasn't real, to Susan it was as beautiful as an authentic fireplace, maybe more so because Ralph built it.

She and Ralph bought electric birch logs that glowed and crackled when switched on. At the end of a tiring day, when the children were sleeping, it was peaceful to curl up on the couch with her head on Ralph's lap. They listened to soft music while dim lights from the electric logs cast an amber glow throughout the room.

After Ralph died, the house no longer felt right to Susan. It was *their* home, not *hers*. Without Ralph, the house seemed too large. Then one by one, the boys married and moved. Finally only she and Laura remained.

She wanted to move away, too. But where? Across town or across the country? Miami was in the midst of cultural upheaval as countless immigrants entered the city. Riots, drugs, and crime were escalating. It seemed to Susan that everyone she knew was leaving. She thought about leaving, too.

A few years earlier, a close friend had moved to a neighboring state. Friends since high school days, she suggested Susan consider moving there, too. Susan visited her, loved the area, and agreed.

The wheels of the move spun into action. First Susan applied for a leave of absence from her job. Then she rented an apartment a block from her friend's home.

Susan was optimistic. She thought the move would be a positive step. Besides, she reasoned, if she regretted her decision, she could always return. Her job was waiting for her, and she purposely didn't sell her house. She *knew* that, if she didn't like the new area, the lease was invalid after a year. She could renew it or discontinue it and return to Miami.

Her old life was over. She had finally accepted Ralph's death. She wanted the opportunity for a renewed, different life. But fear got in the way. For months before she made the decision, the question to move or not to move zigzagged in and out of her thoughts. Go? Don't go? What should she do?

She was no longer happy where she was, that she knew. Finally she decided to act on her friend's suggestion. She hoped that she wasn't making a mistake. But unless she took the risk, how would she know?

Susan glanced at her watch, picked up her purse, and headed through the door. She wanted to visit the cemetery before the movers came. She paused to break a gardenia from the flowering bush beside the door. Ralph always loved gardenias. She'd bring one to the cemetery. As she drove through the early morning traffic, the fragrant flower perfumed the air.

She knelt on the soft grass that covered Ralph's grave. Then she put the gardenia in the copper urn attached to the marker. Lost in thought, she brushed a wisp of hair from her eyes.

"I never wanted to leave you," she whispered, "but I have to move on. Everything has changed so. I know you understand. Somehow, you always understood. I need to go, but I'm scared, Ralph." She shrugged her shoulders and continued, "but then I've always been a scaredy cat, haven't I?"

Susan raised her head and smiled. "I guess some things never change. But I *am* getting stronger, Ralph. I think you'd be pleased at how strong I've become. I know I'm going to be all right. I really am."

Then she turned. Head held high, she walked to her car.

Joyce

I held it in my hands, turning it over carefully. It

wasn't large nor thick. *But it was mine!* On its spine, in neat black letters, was my name: Joyce J. Tyra. Now I could believe it. *I've written a book.*

I felt pleased, fulfilled. Tonight there were no shadows; they were chased by happiness. My thoughts turned to Ed. *This book is for you, Honey,* I whispered to myself. *Your specialness won't be forgotten. You'll live on in our children's and my memories for as long as we live.*

I glanced around the room. Tears of pleasure clouded my gaze. Most of the people I cared for were here. My sister was cutting the cake, putting slices on plates, and passing it to my friends. My son Mike was smiling and pouring champagne into crystal goblets. Tom, my absent son, had just called from his military station in Germany to extend his love.

It was a party and I was the guest of honor. My family and closest friends were here to share my joy. Each of these people were dear to me and each of their names are included in the pages of my book. Tonight I would thank them again for the love and emotional support they provided after Ed died. Then I would give each a copy of *Until Death Do Us Part.*

Karen, my daughter, slipped her arm around my waist. Radiant and smiling, she handed a little package to me.

I untied the ribbon and removed the silver paper. A miniature golden typewriter gleamed against black velvet.

"To add to your charm bracelet, Mom," Karen said. "Tom, Mike, and I wanted to give you something special to remind you of the hours you sat glued to your typewriter. Do you like it?"

I held the little charm. "Like it?," I said. "I *love* it. It's perfect. It's very special."

Mike's voice rose above the murmur of laughter and talking. "Everyone, may I have your attention, please? I'd like to make a toast."

I smiled and looked at the faces of my family and friends.

Then Mike raised his goblet. "We love you, Mom," he said, "and we're very proud of you."

My voice was scarcely a whisper. "Thank you," I said. "Thank you, everyone." Closing my eyes, I added, "And thank you, God."

Then came hugs and tears and laughter.

Select Bibliography

Allen, Charles. *When a Marriage Ends*, Old Tappan, N.J.: Fleming H. Revell Co., 1986.

Fisher, Bruce. *Rebuilding*, San Luis Obispo, Calif.: Impact Publishers, 1981.

Fisher, Esther. *Divorce: The New Freedom*, New York: Harper & Row Publishers, 1974.

Hunt, Bernice and Morton Hunt. *The Divorce Experience*, New York: McGraw Hill Book Company, 1977.

Jensen, Marilyn. *Formerly Married*, Philadelphia: Bridge-books: The Westminster Press, 1983.

Krantzler, Mel. *Creative Divorce*, New York: Signet, 1973.

The Author

When widowed suddenly at forty-five, Joyce Tyra joined thousands of newly widowed and divorced women who each year must start over in mid-life. Feeling devastated and lost, Joyce eventually turned her grief and disillusionment into happiness again.

Joyce earned a B.A. in journalism from Florida Atlantic University and an M.S. in English from Florida International University. She teaches high school in the Miami area.

After writing *Until Death Do Us Part* (Nashville, Tenn.: Randall House, 1989), an inspirational book for widows, Joyce learned that widows aren't the only ones who are lonely and feel alienated when marriage ends. Divorcées do, too. Whether a mate is lost to death or a divorce court, widows and divorcées must pick up the pieces of their lives and start over. In *Starting Over*, Joyce reaches out to all who have lost mates.

Joyce is mother of Thomas (1961), Michael (1963), and Karen (1966). She is a member of Sunrise Presbyterian Church in Miami.